Progressive Patterns

A Man's World

Adult Colouring Book

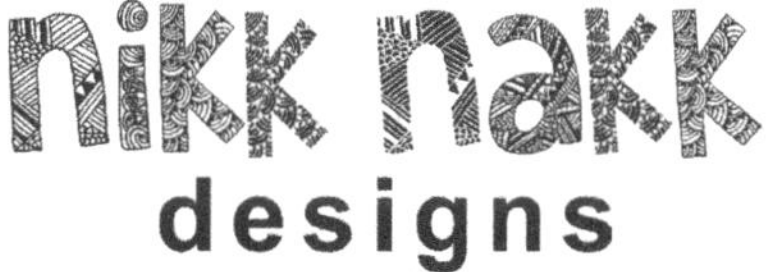

designs

Progressive Patterns - A Man's World - Adult Colouring Book

Copyright 2015 by nikk nakk designs
Created by Niki Palmer and Ros Tulleners
Illustrated by Stuart Campbell, Subrata Dutta, Elshan Gurbanov,
Isabelle Patterson, Hasnat Rabi, and Ian Torr

First edition 2015

ISBN: 978-1-925422-07-8
www.nikknakkdesigns.com.au

Welcome to Progressive Patterns - A Man's World - Adult Coloring Book - a collection of 30 designs created especially FOR men.

You won't find any flowers, rainbows, unicorns or fluffy kittens in these pages!

Colouring has been proven to be a very effective stress reliever creating a sense of peace and tranquility.

When you are feeling stressed, close out your hectic connected world, turn off your phone and pick up a pencil.

Lose yourself in the moment.

It's so easy to unwind as you focus on the page and JUST ADD COLOUR with coloured pencils, watercolour pencils, felt tips, gel pens, whatever medium you choose - let your imagination run wild.

Each page is printed on one side only, giving you lots of opportunities to experiment with different pens, pencils and tips, using light and heavy pressure for different effects.

There are no rules- forget your kindergarten teacher - you don't even have to stay inside the lines - just let your creative juices flow.

 Before you know it, you will feel calm, renewed and ready to face the world again.

    When your world is feeling a little grey, it time to add some colour to it!

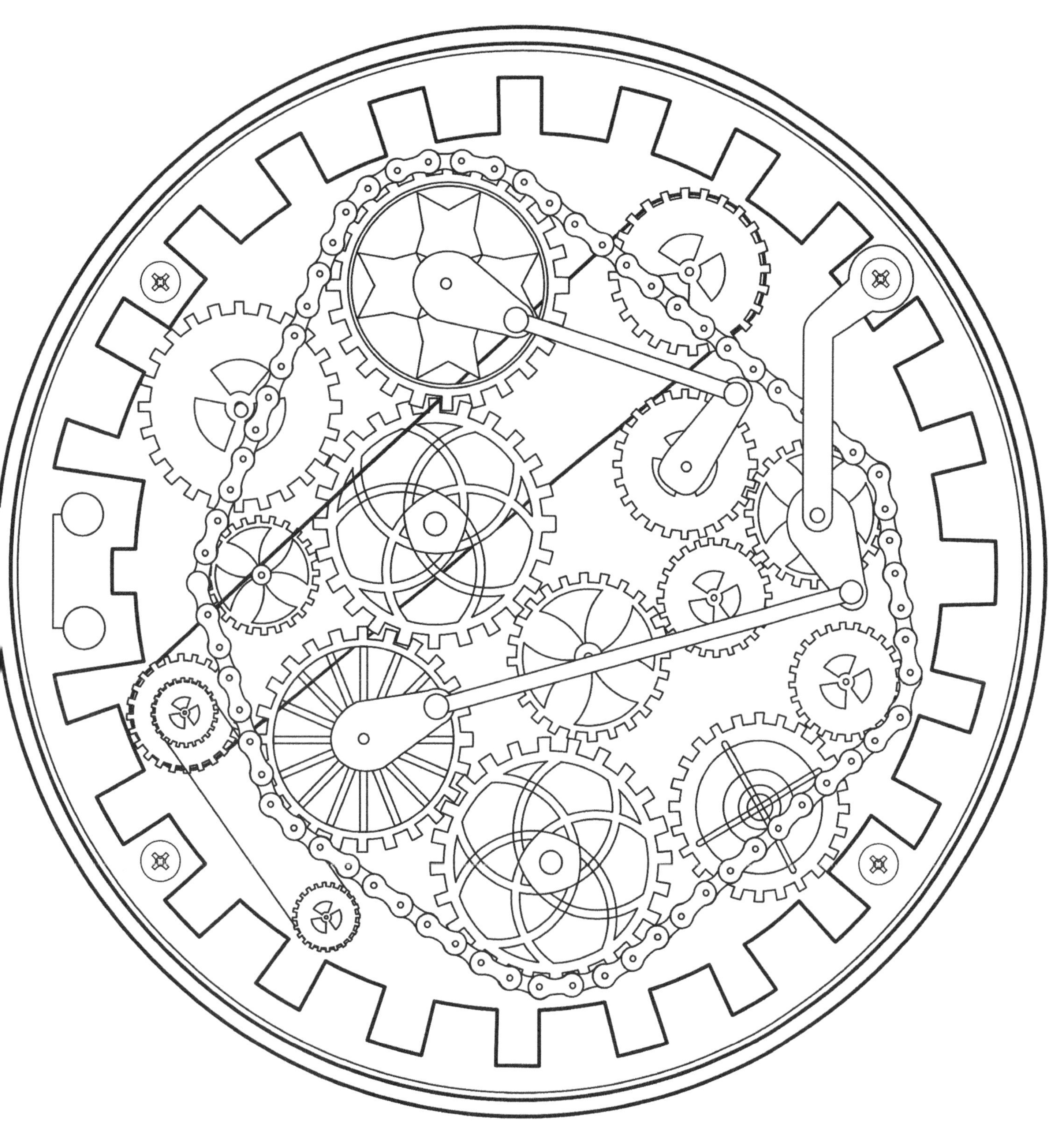

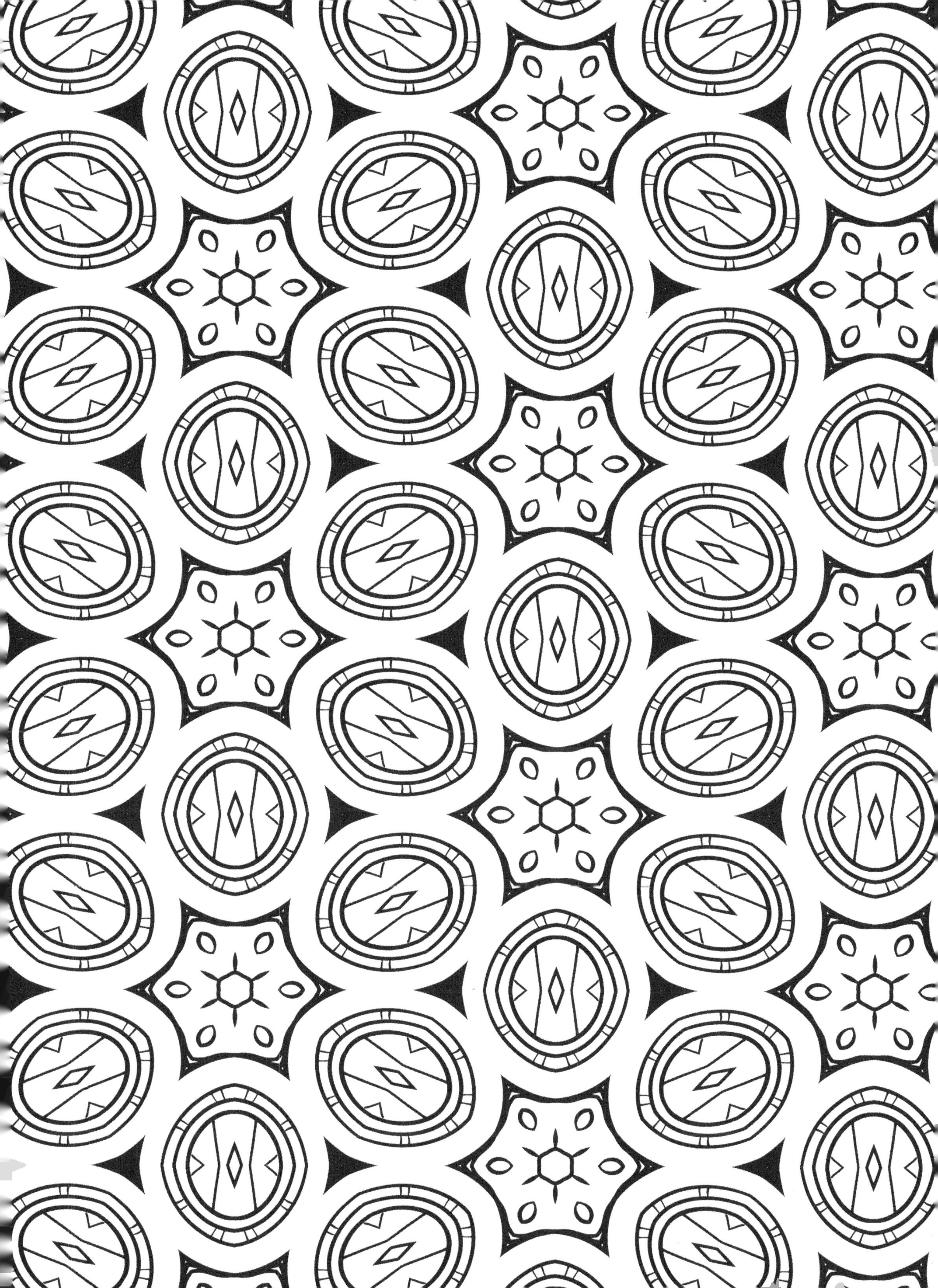

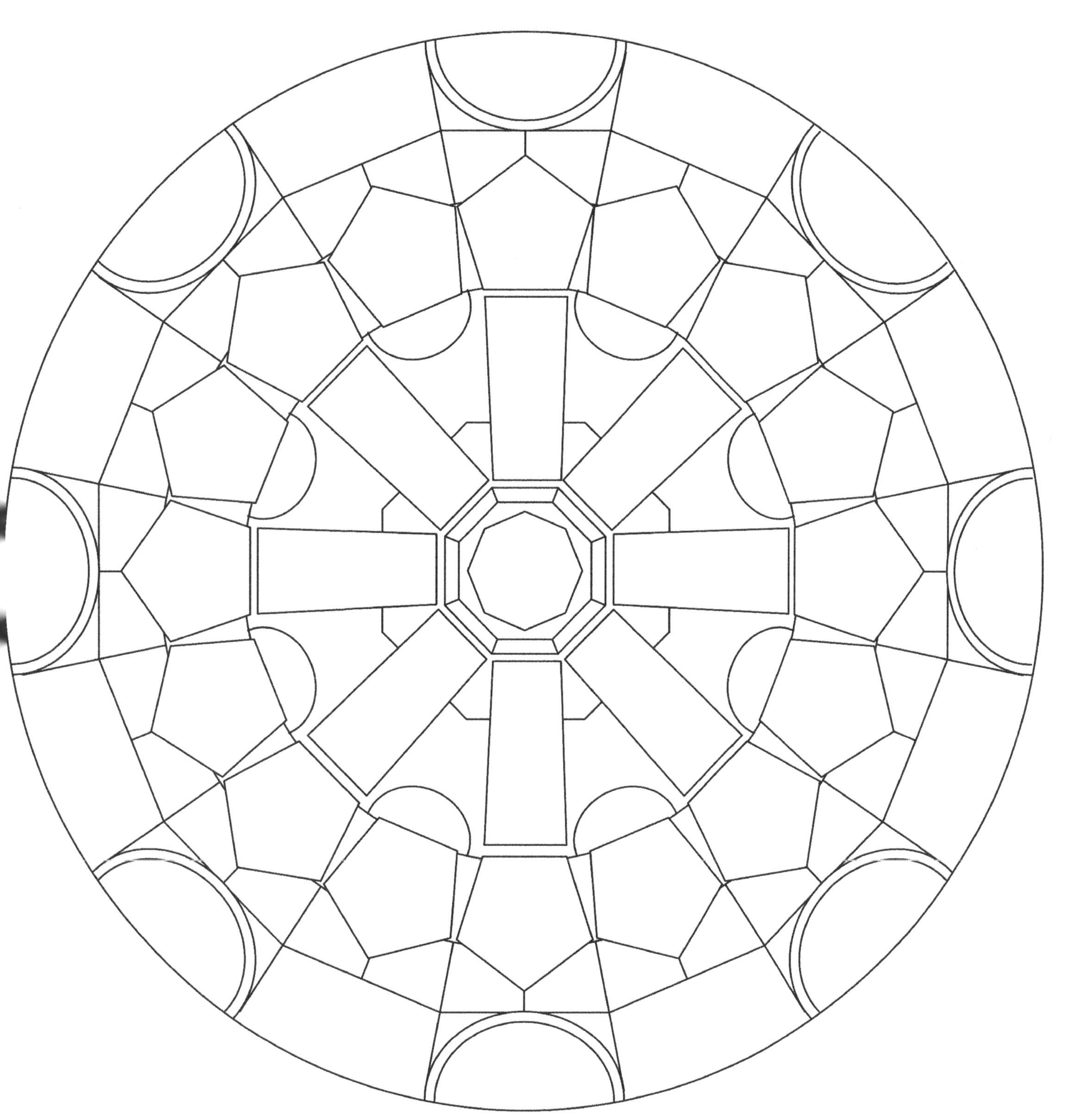

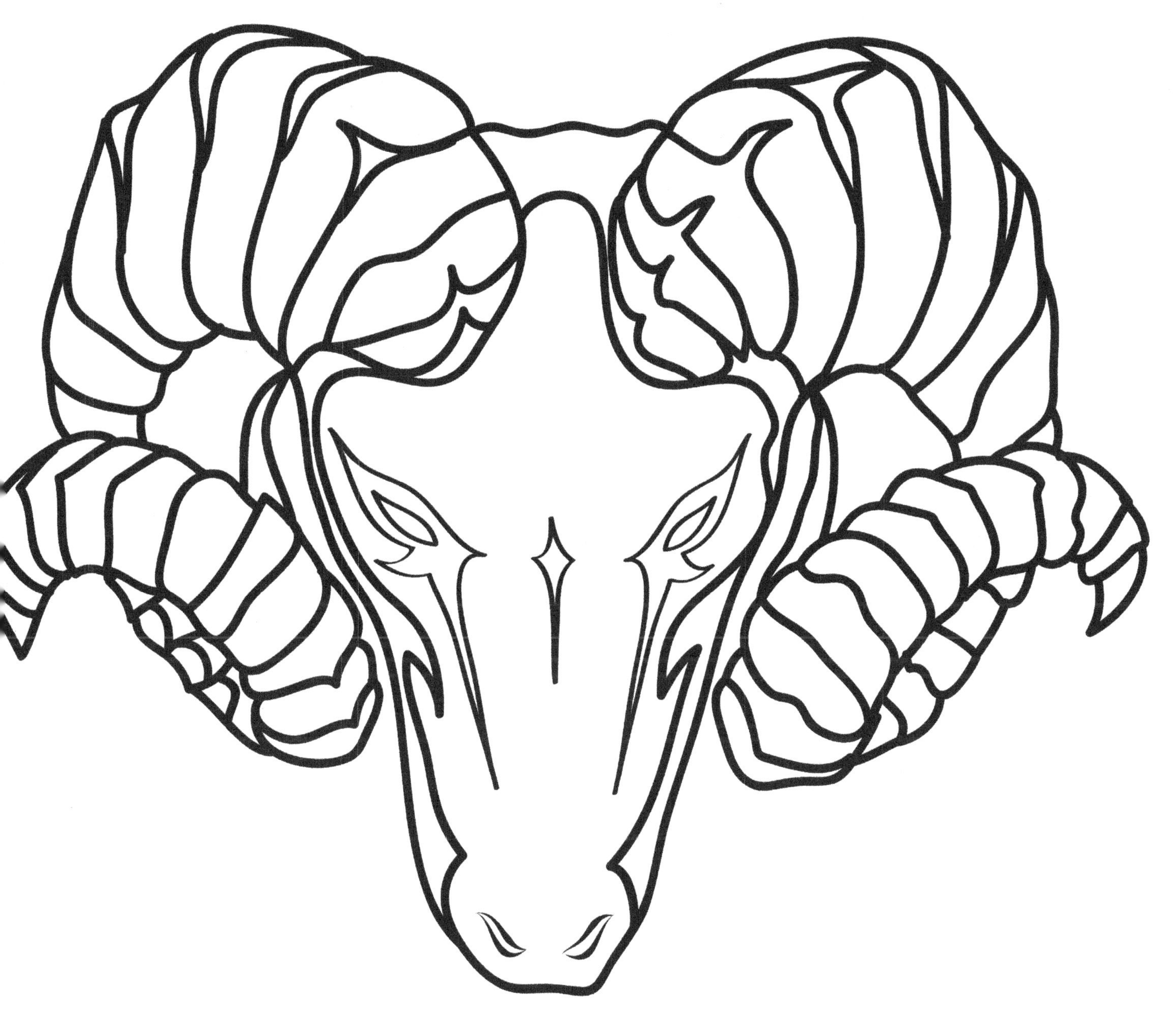

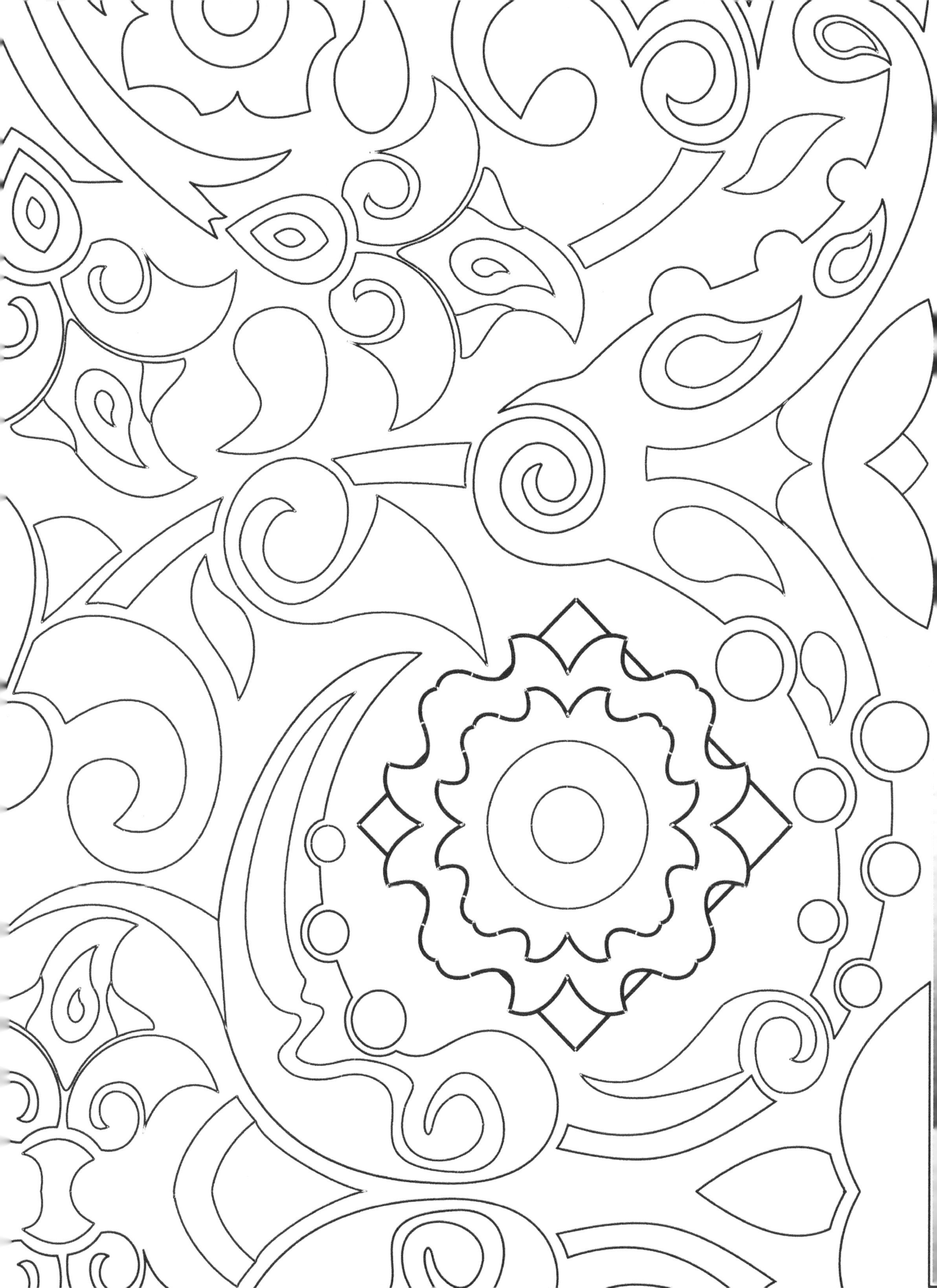

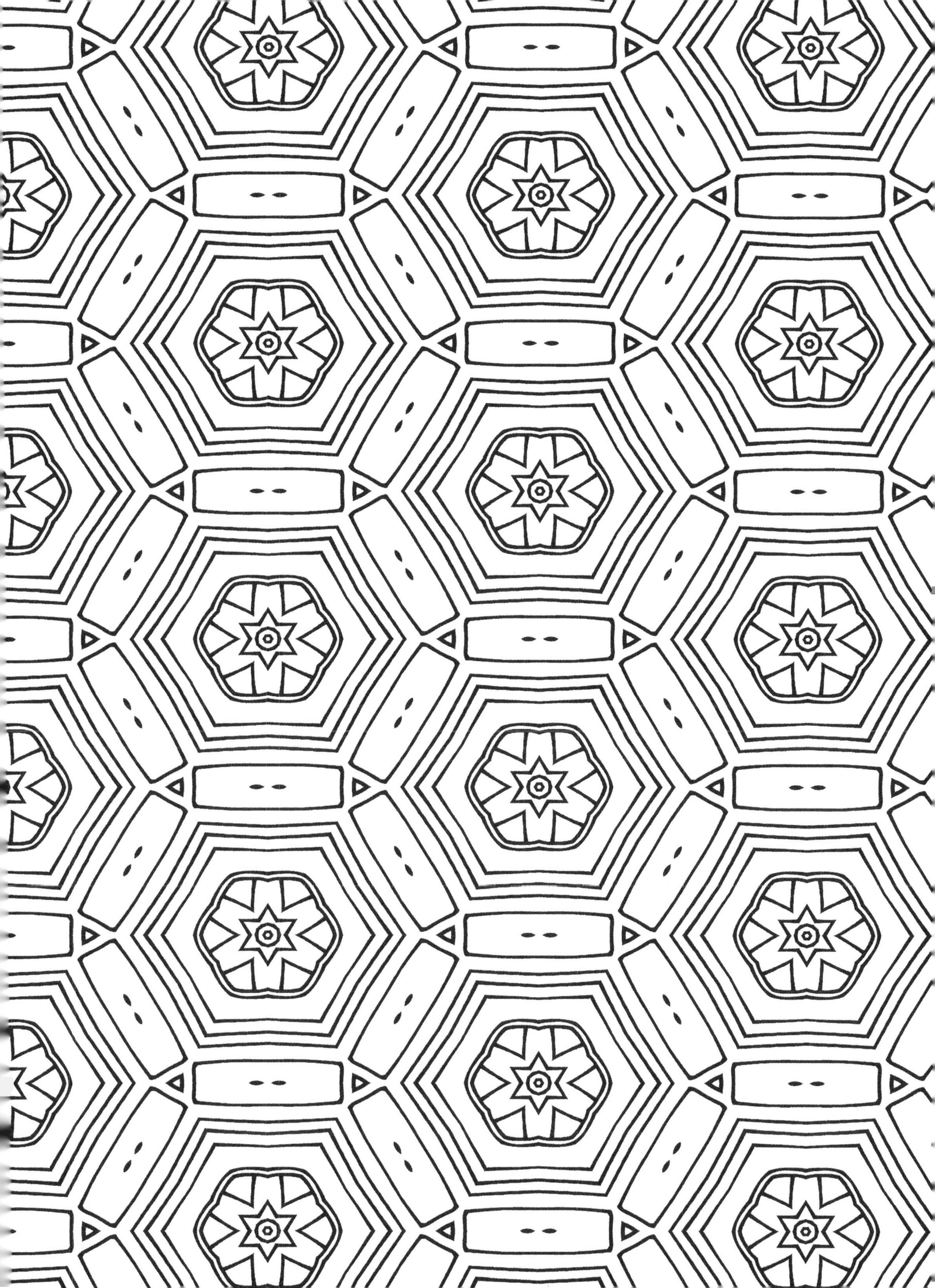

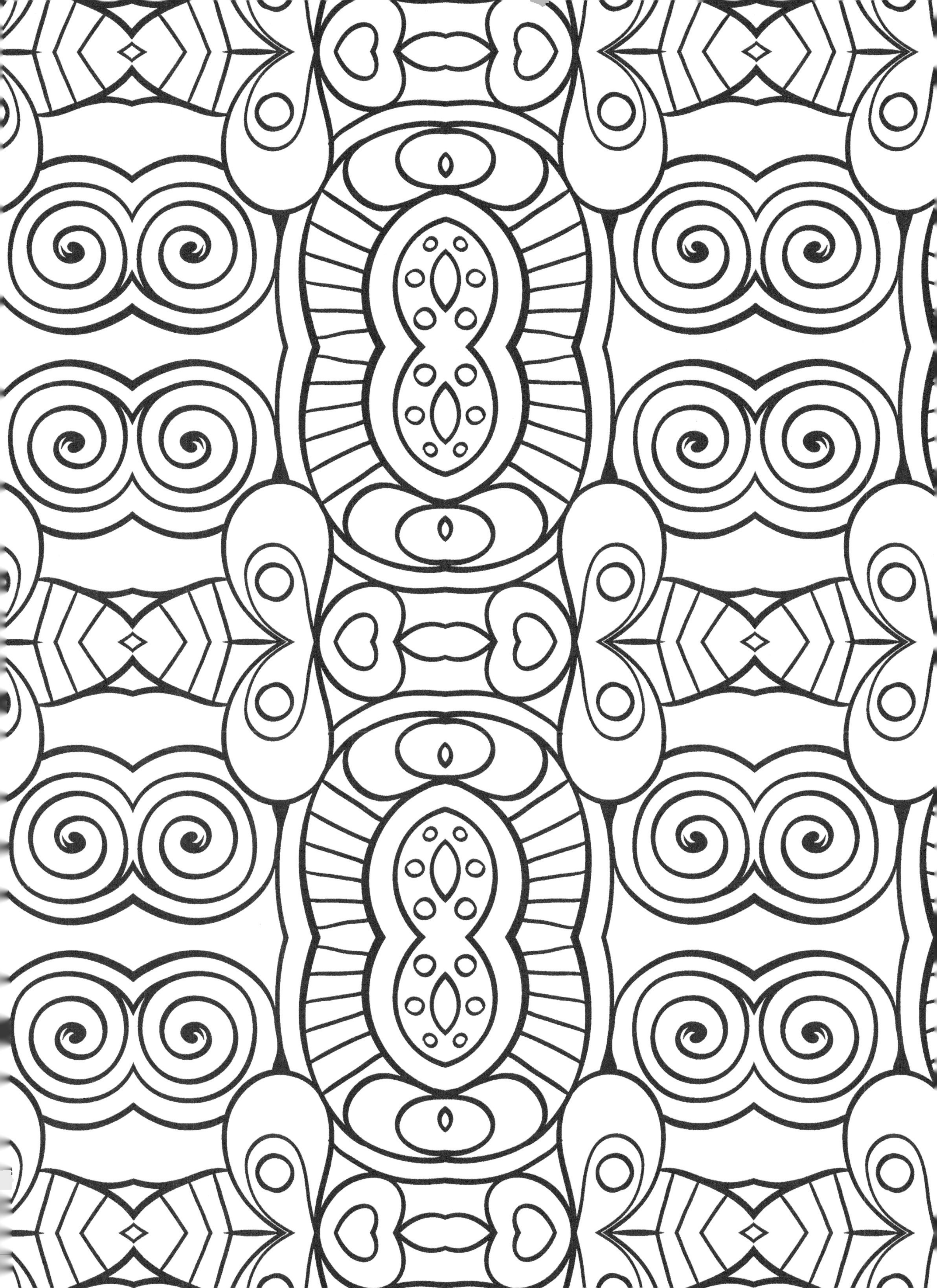

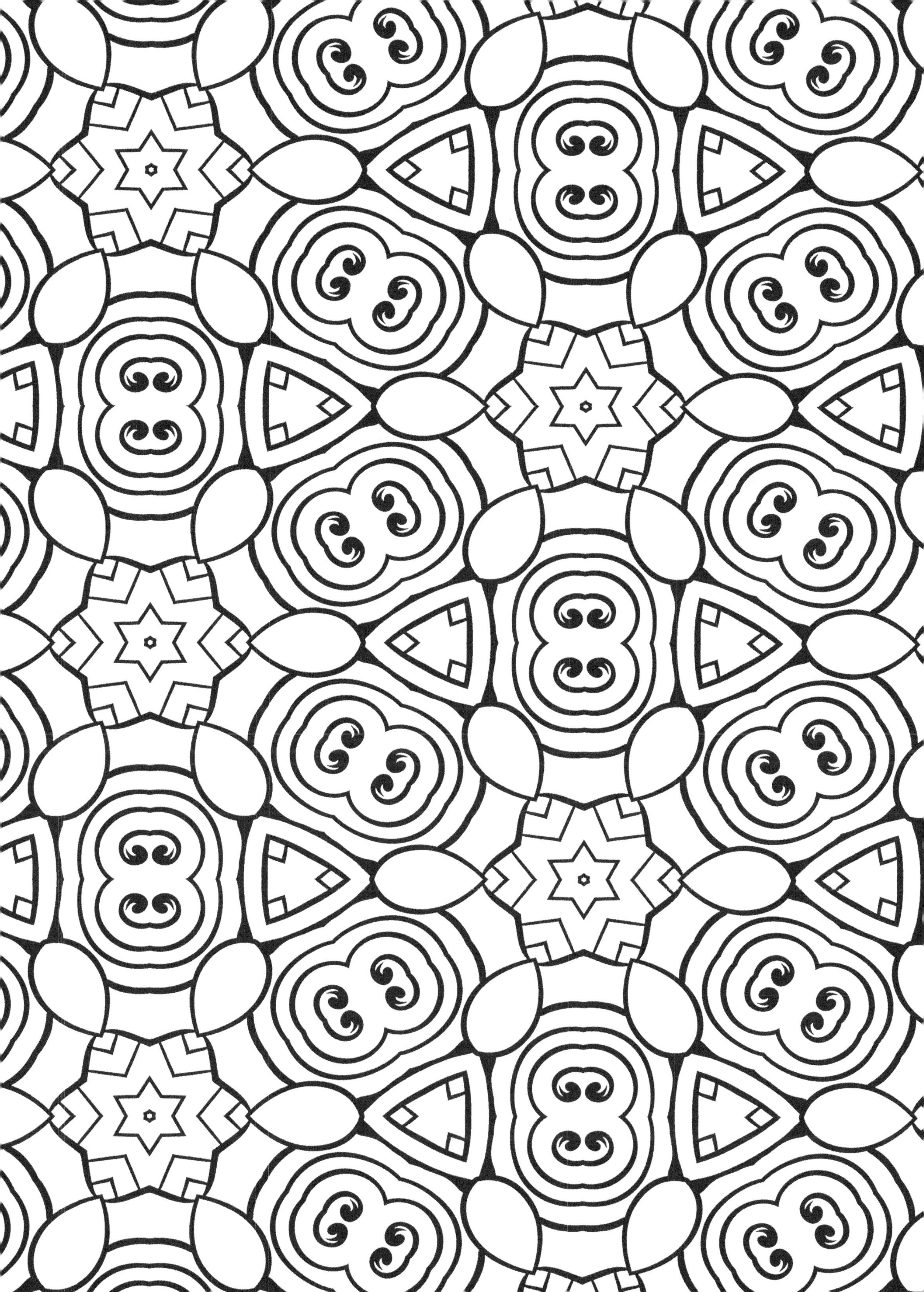

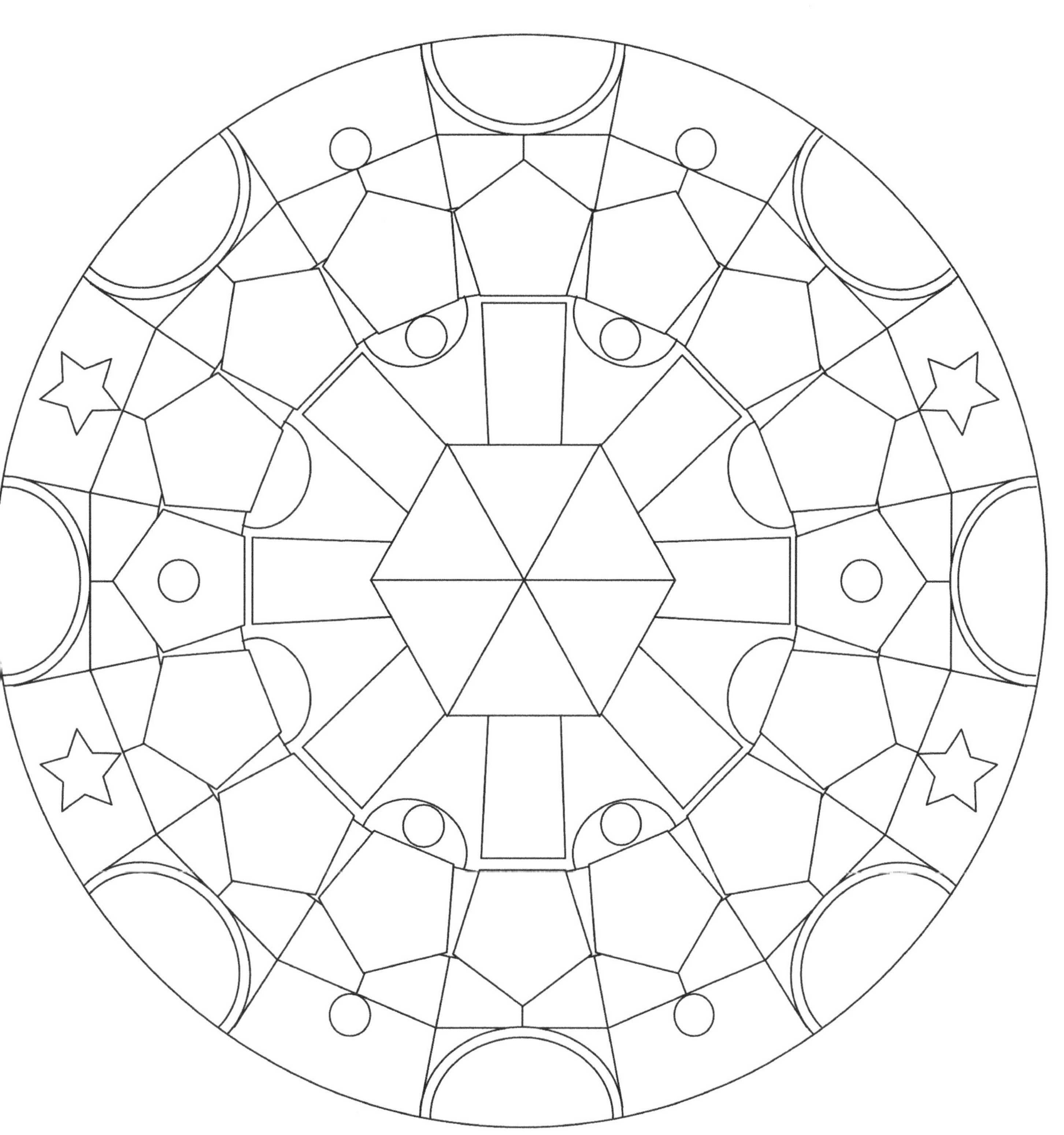

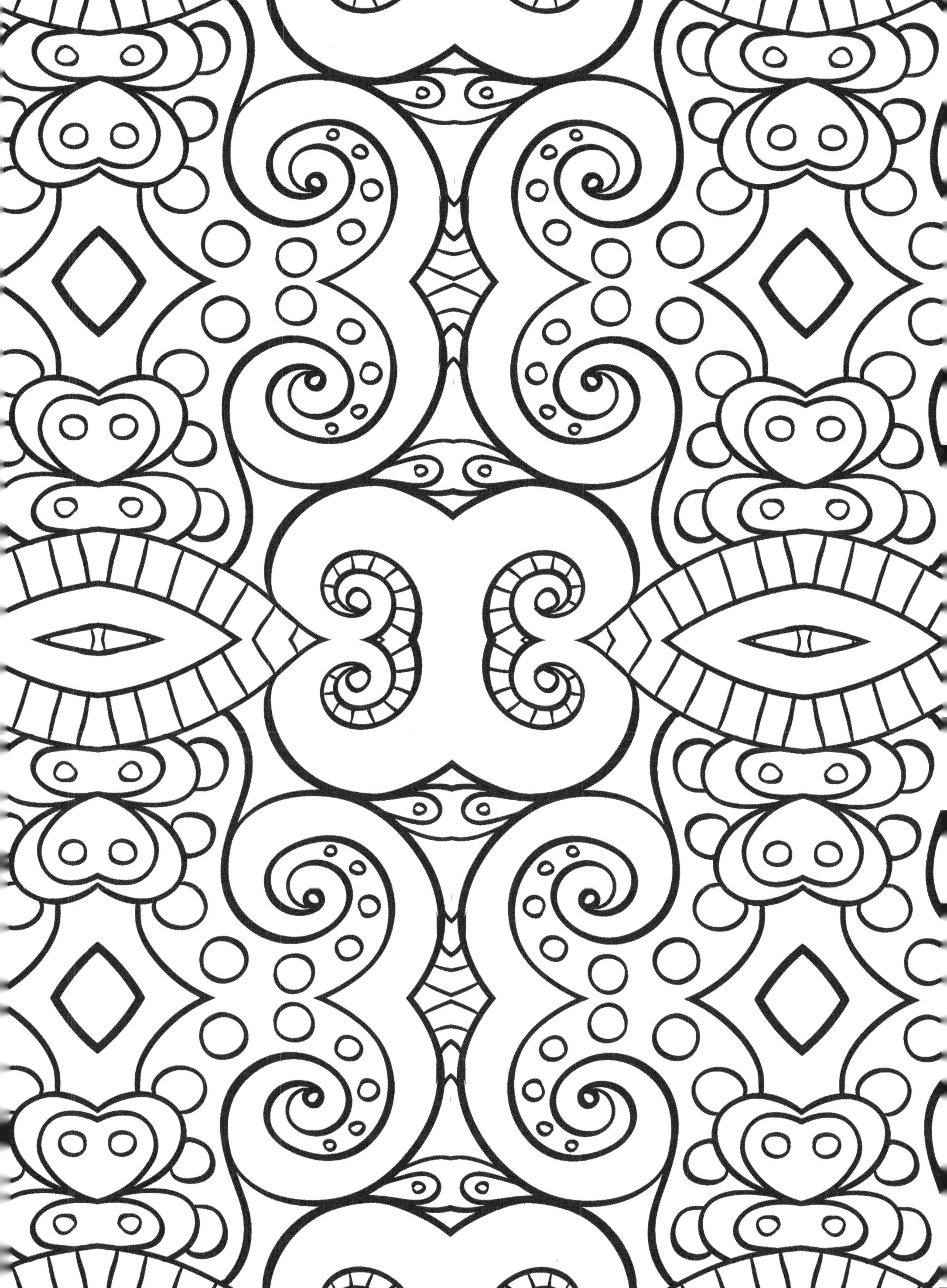

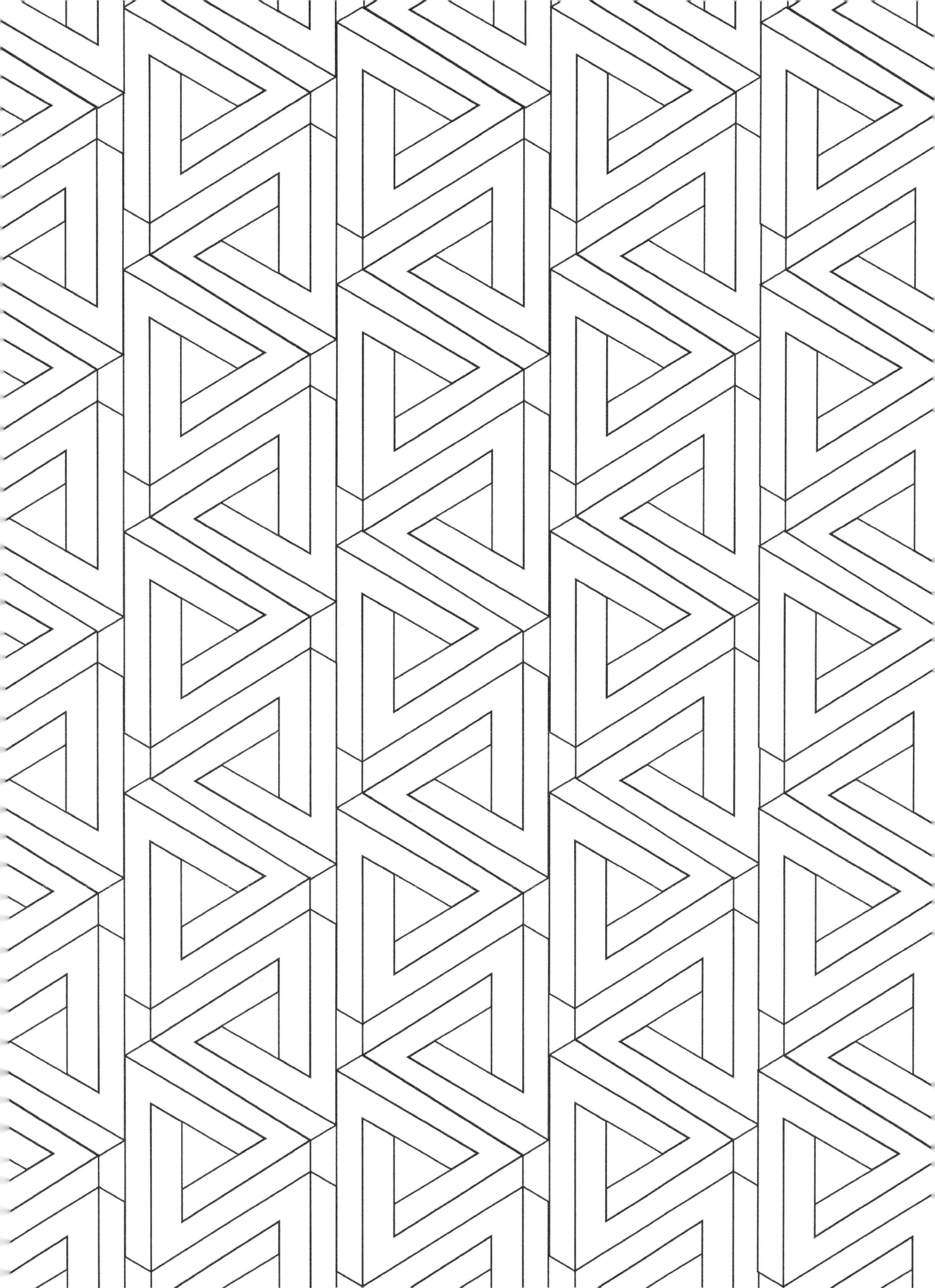

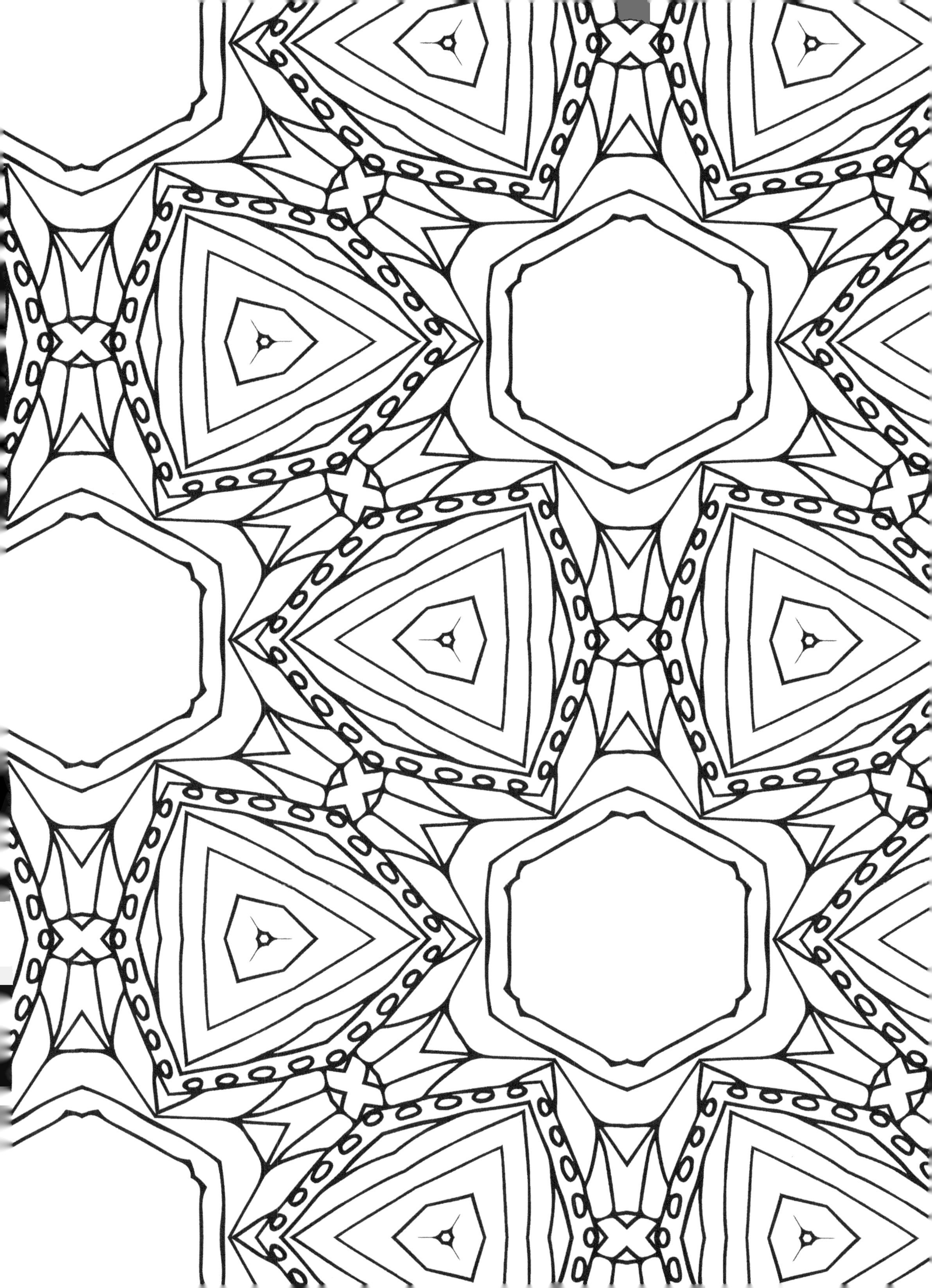

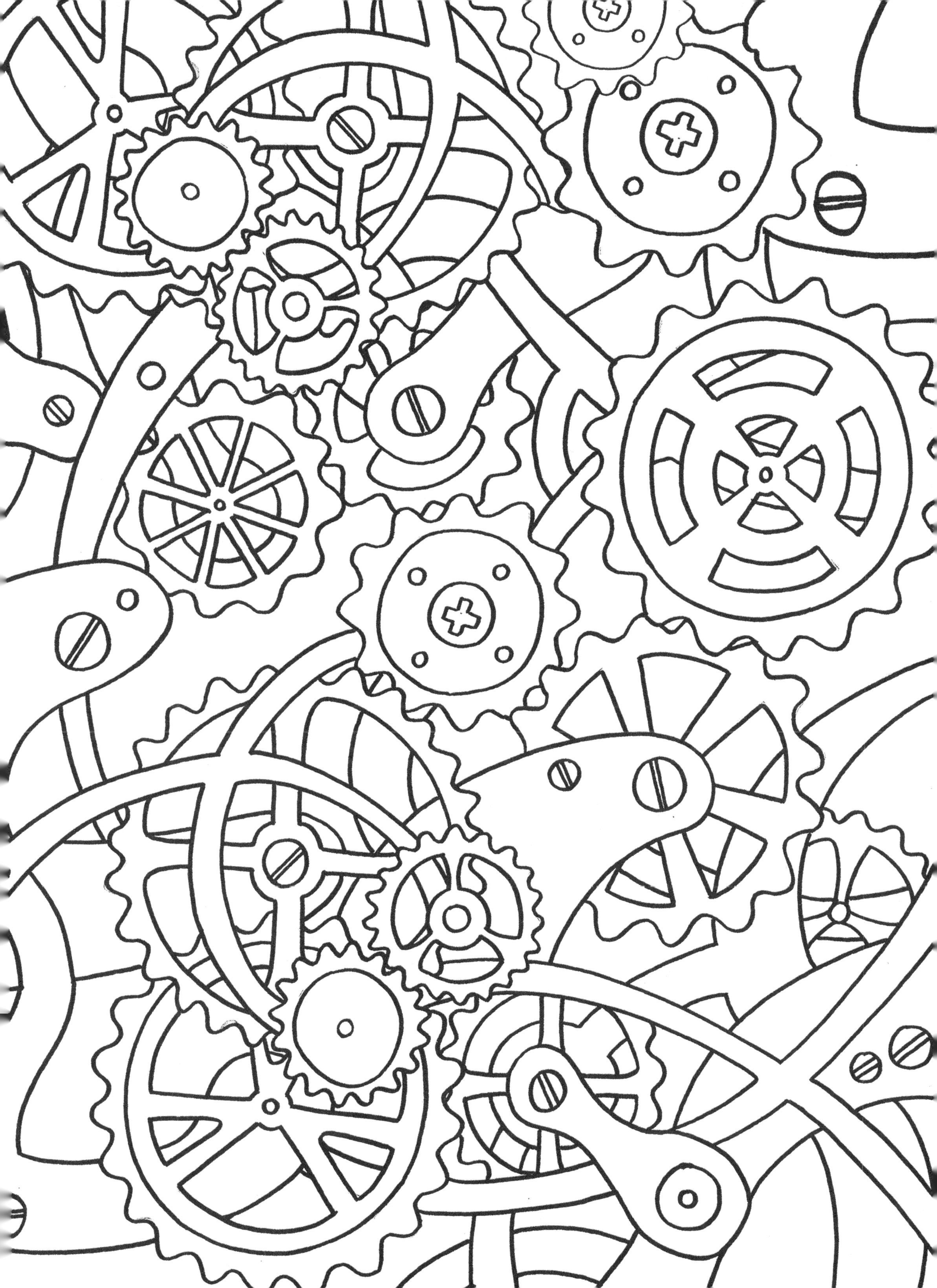

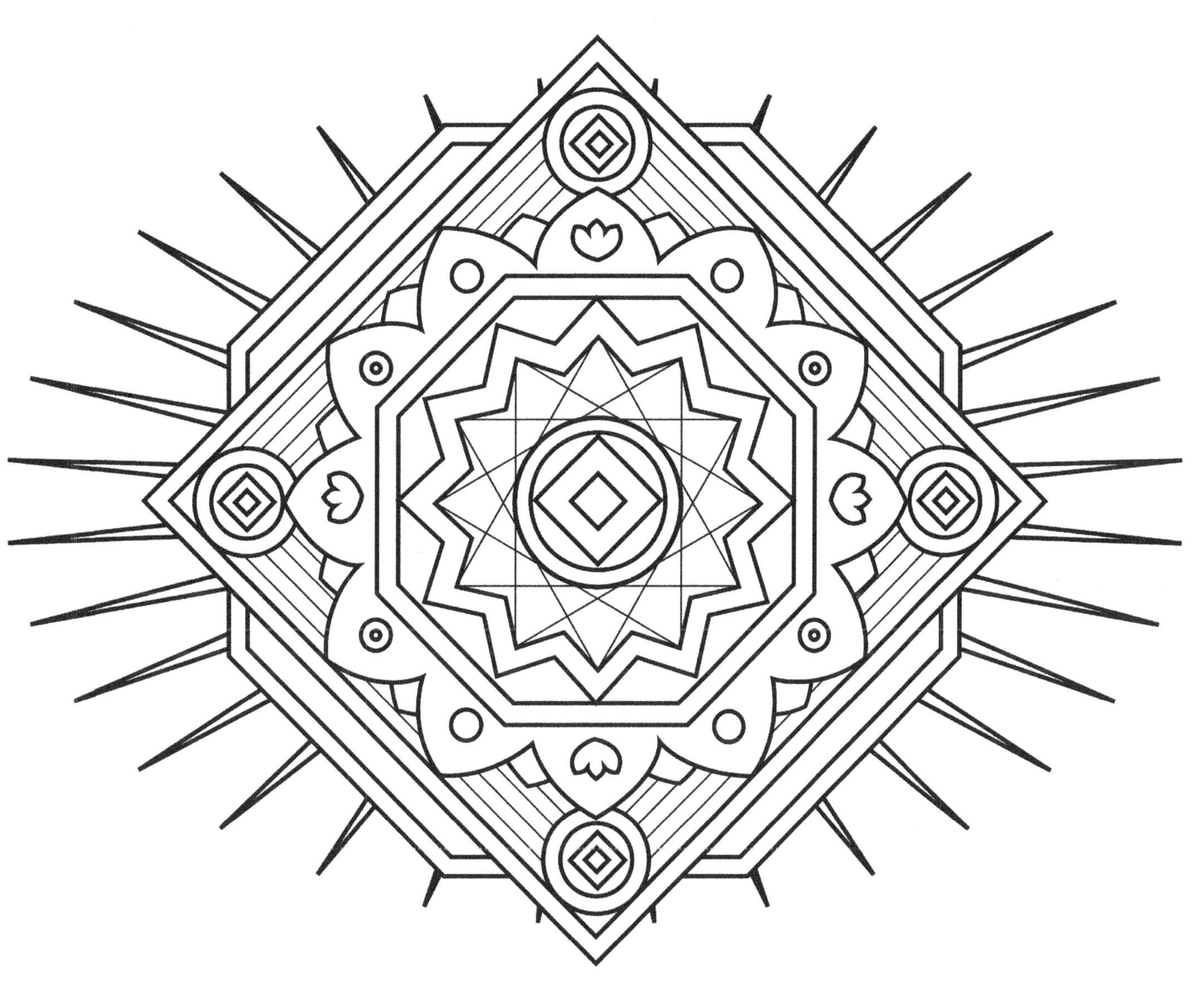

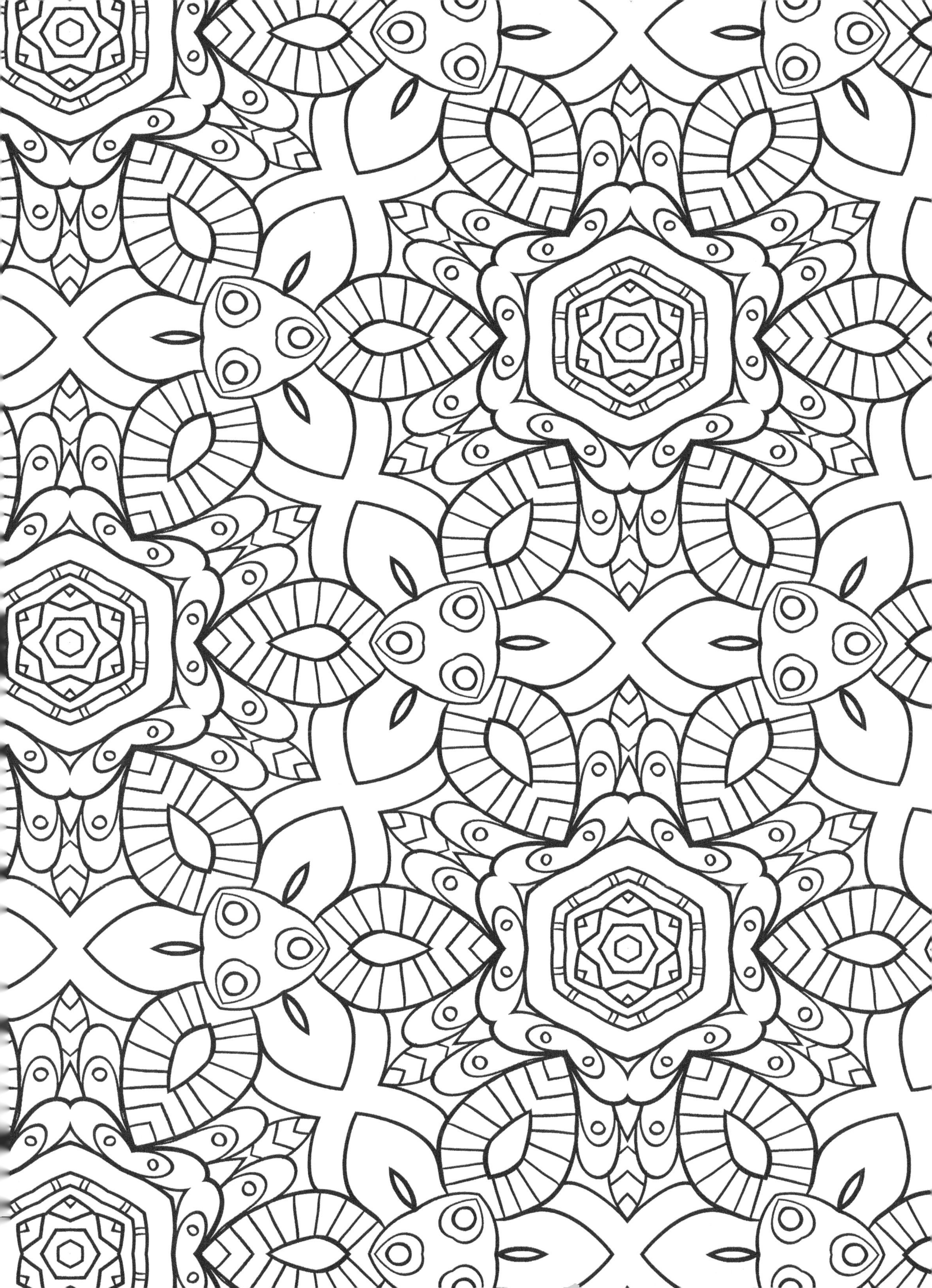

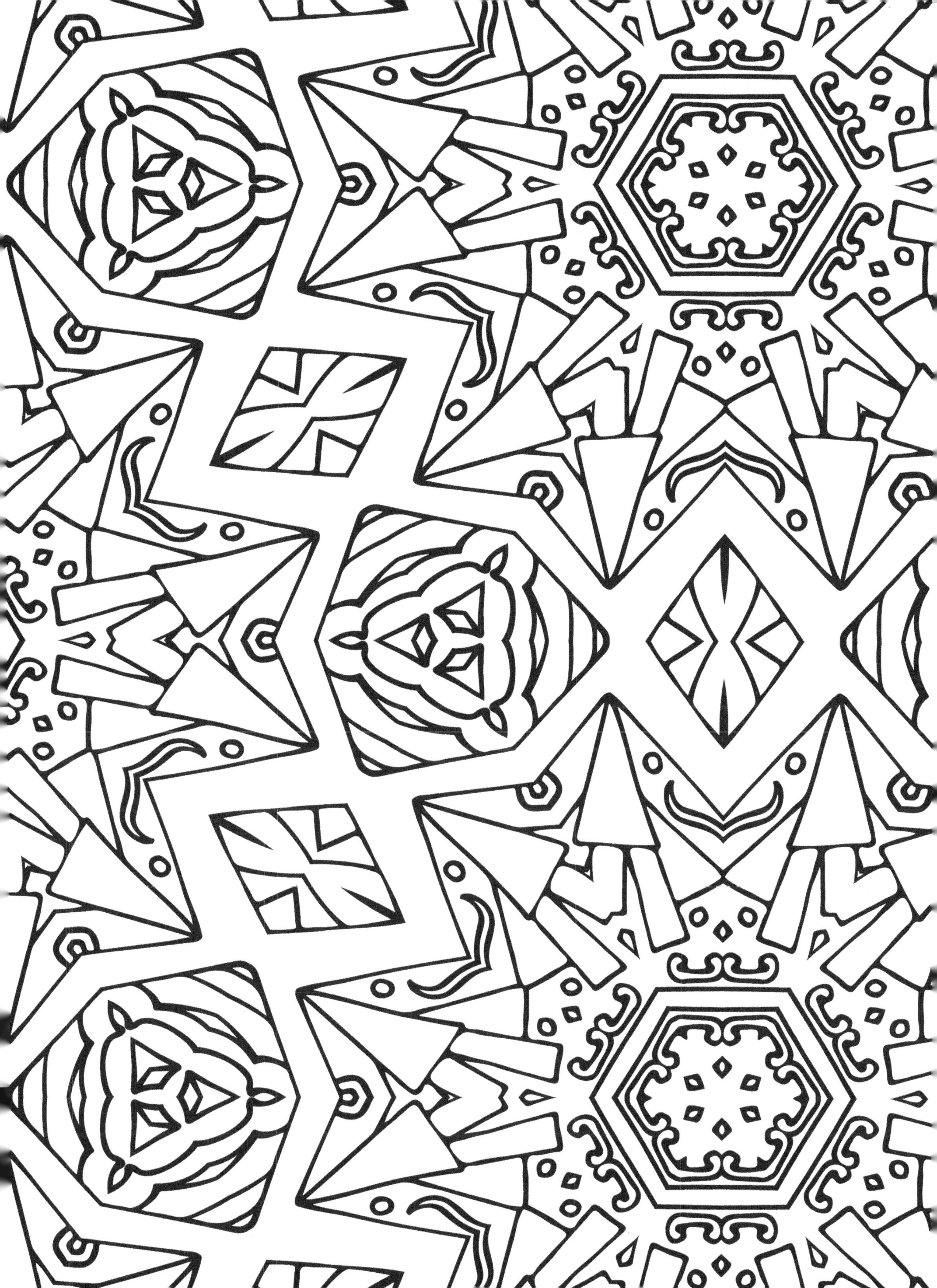

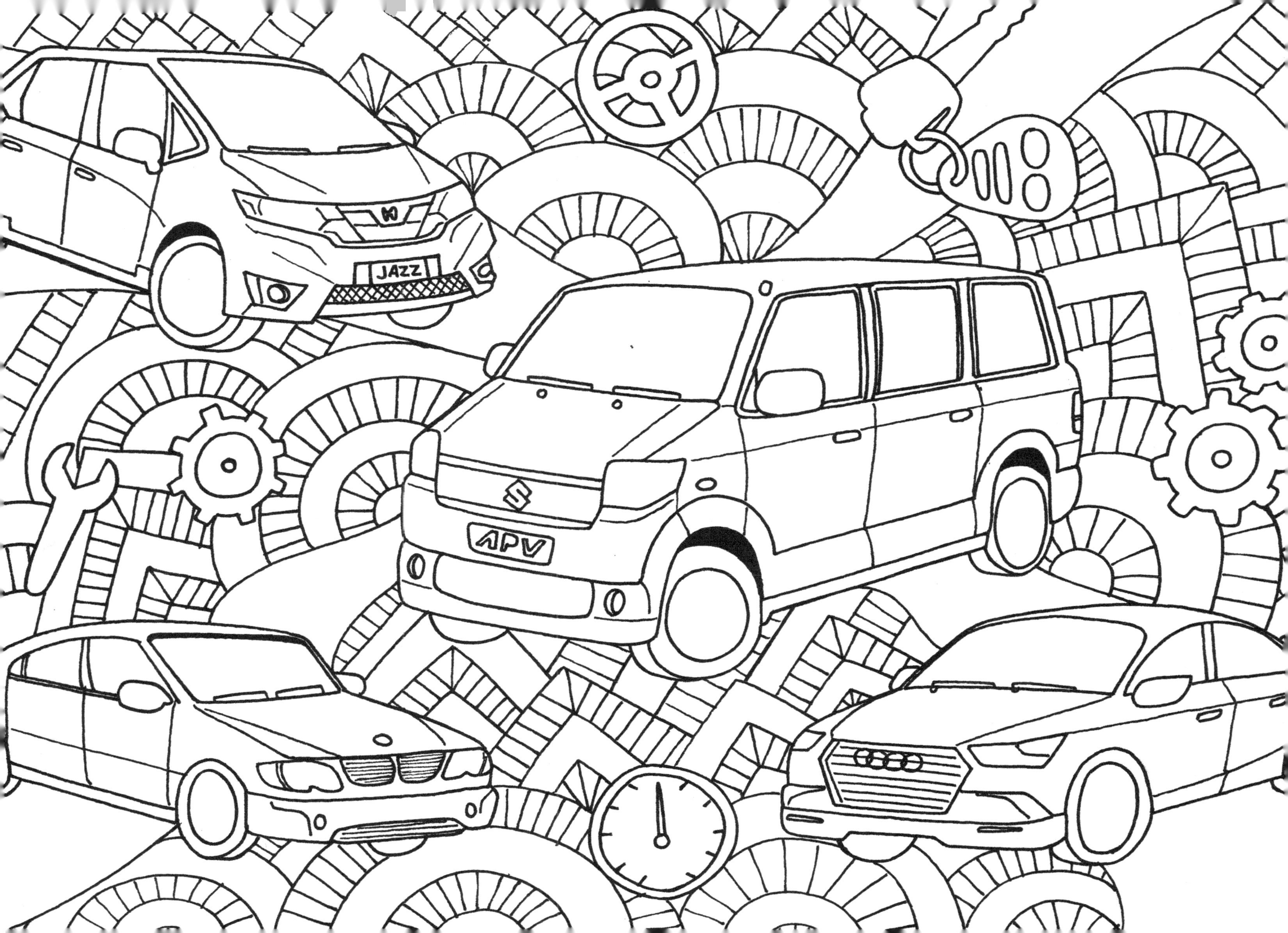

JAZZ
APV

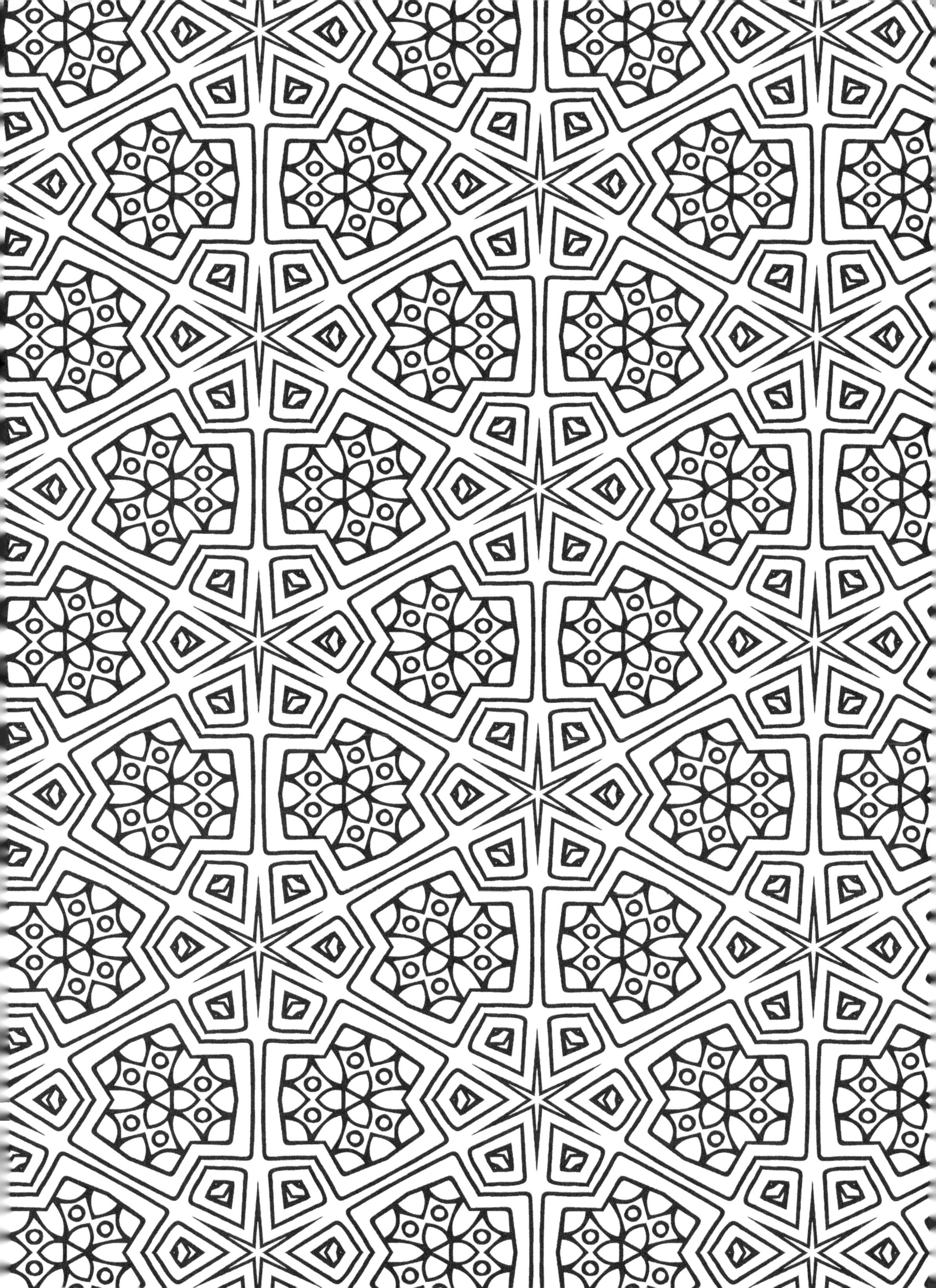

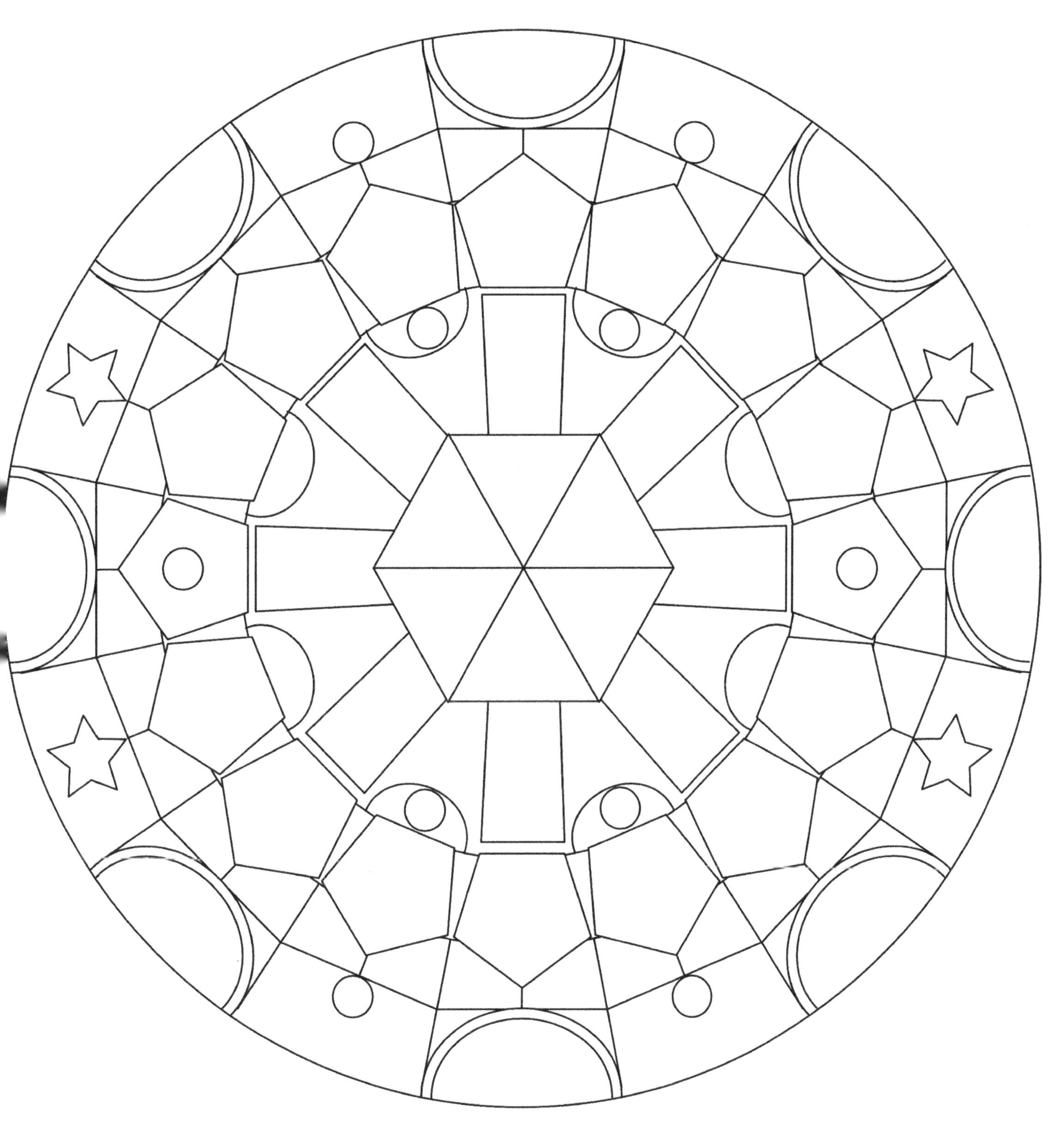

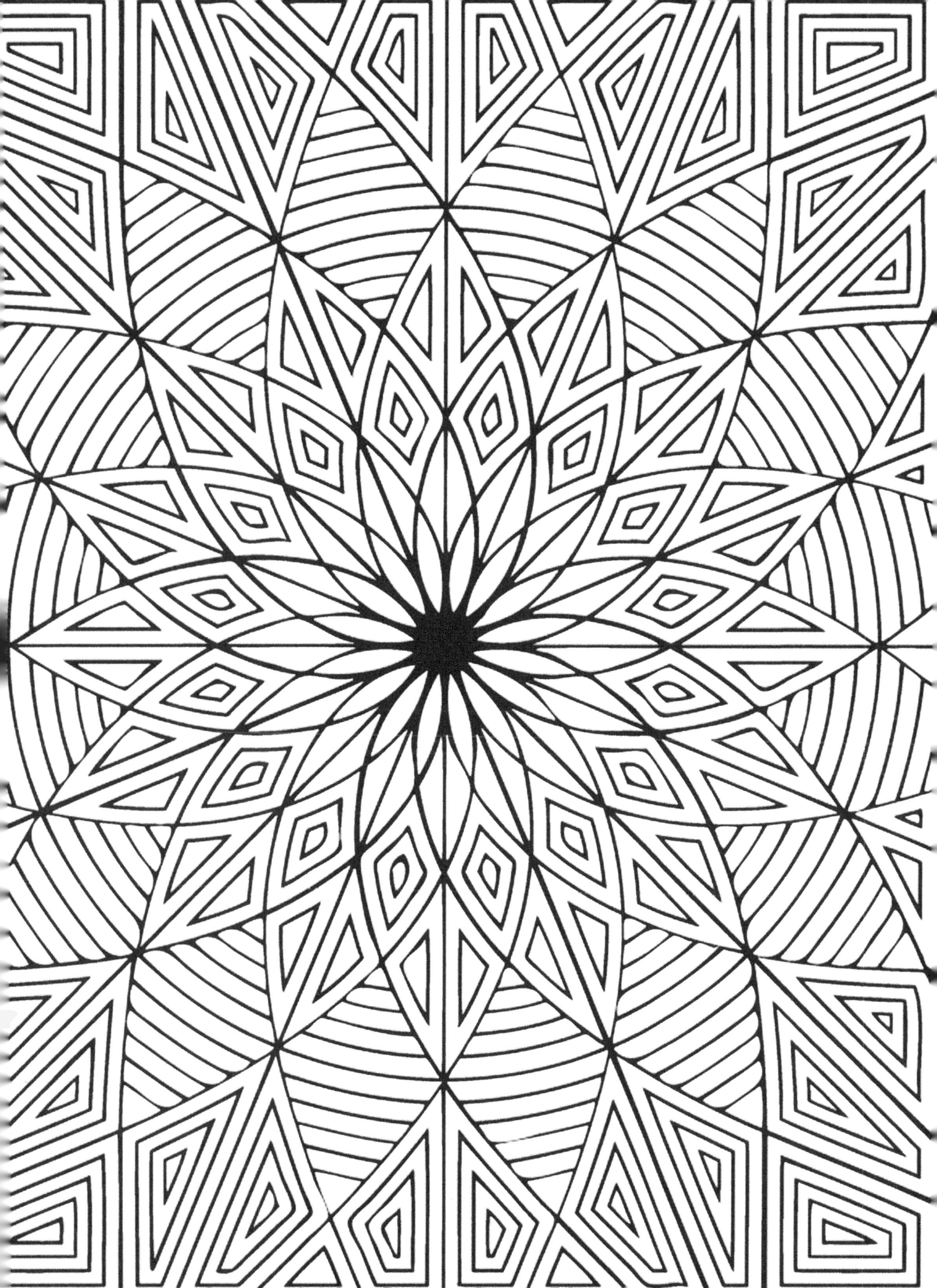

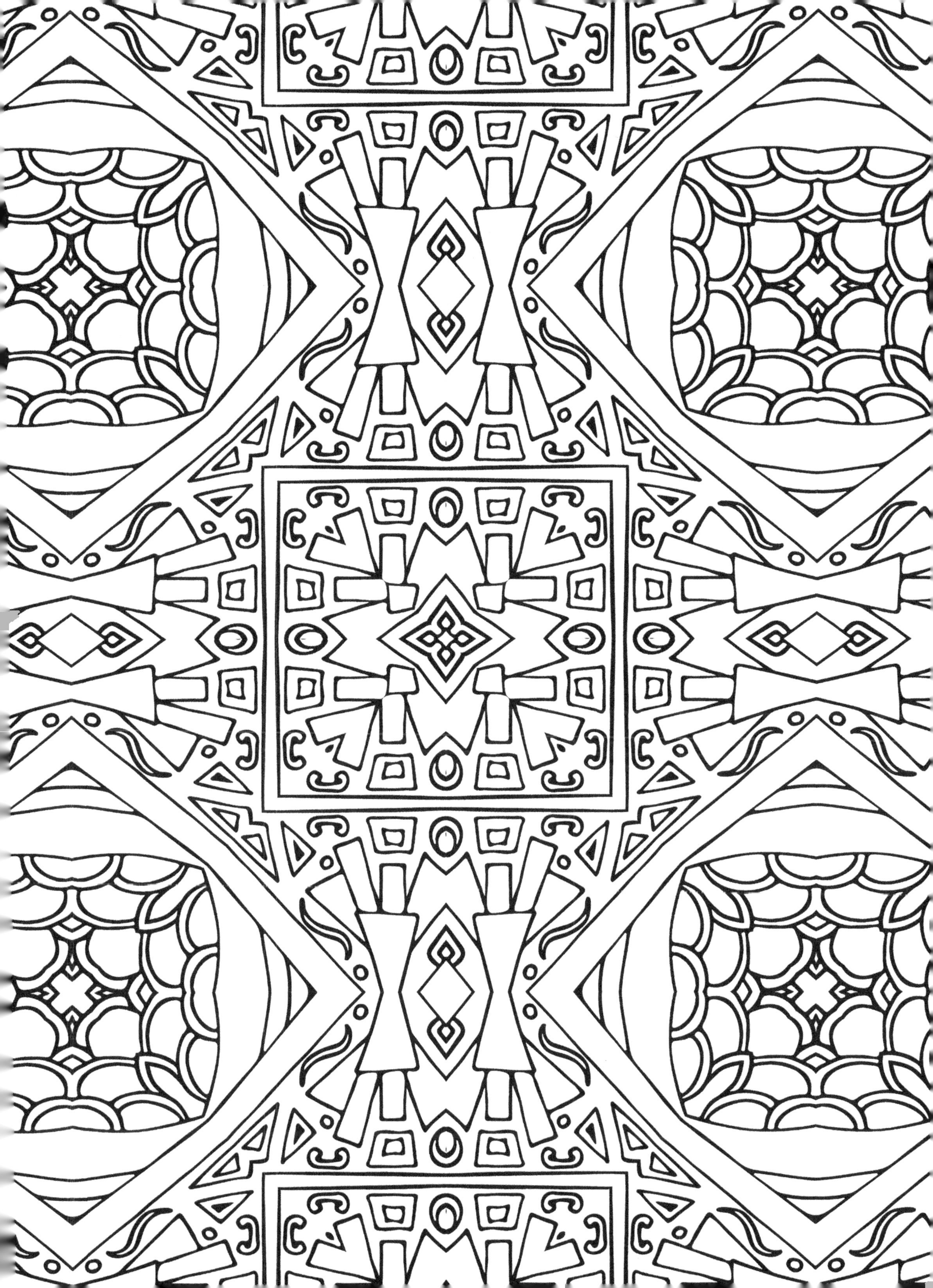

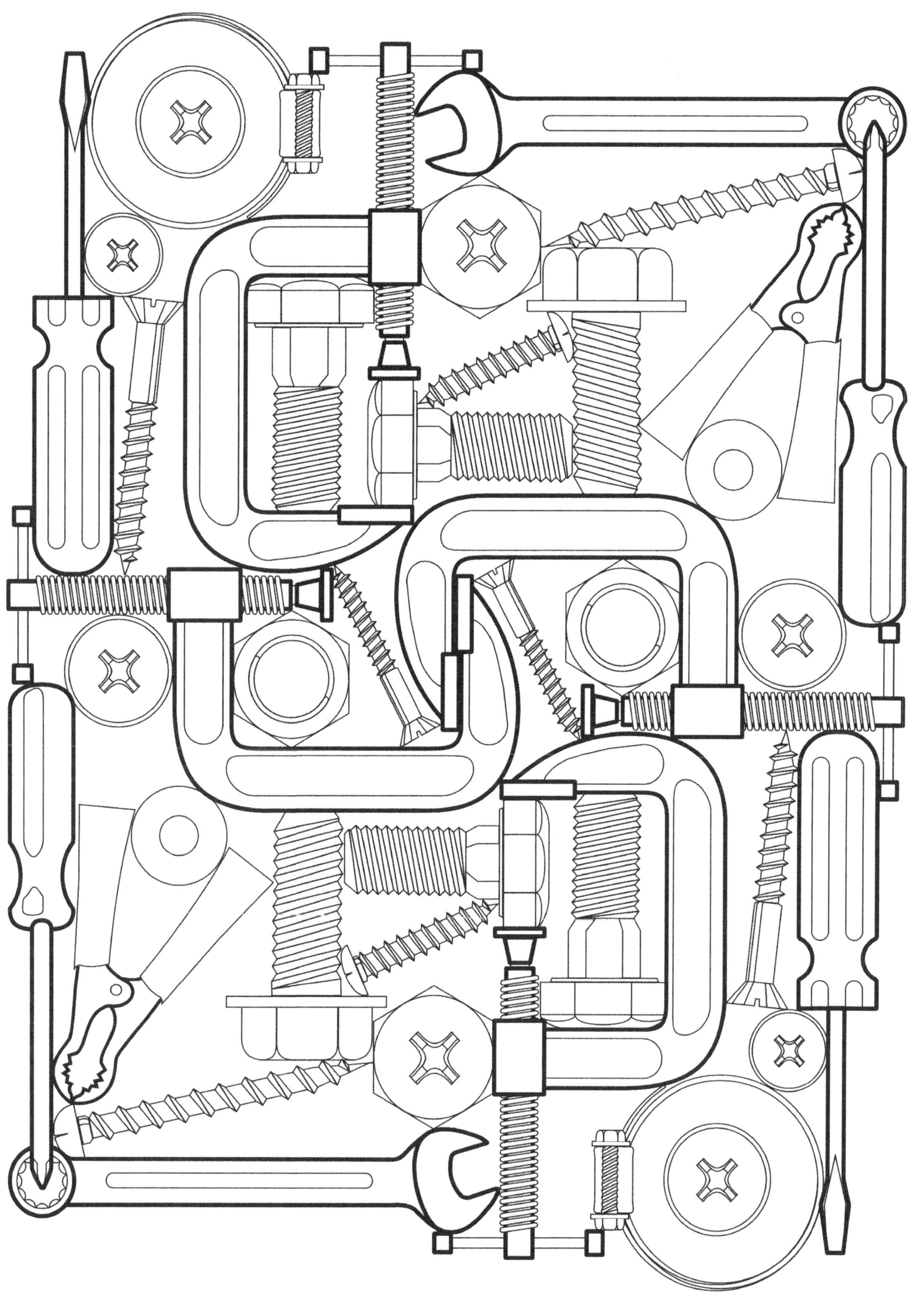

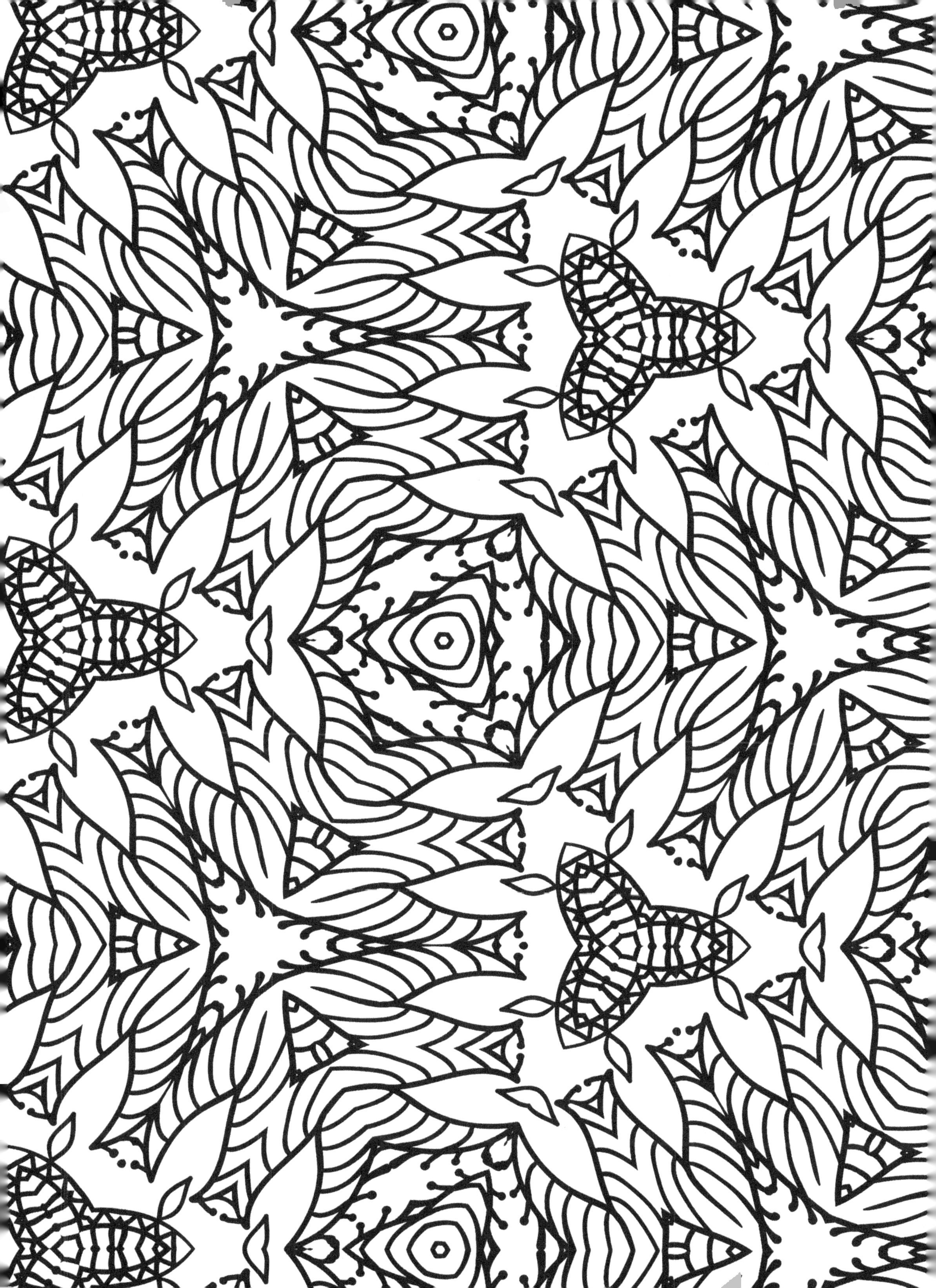

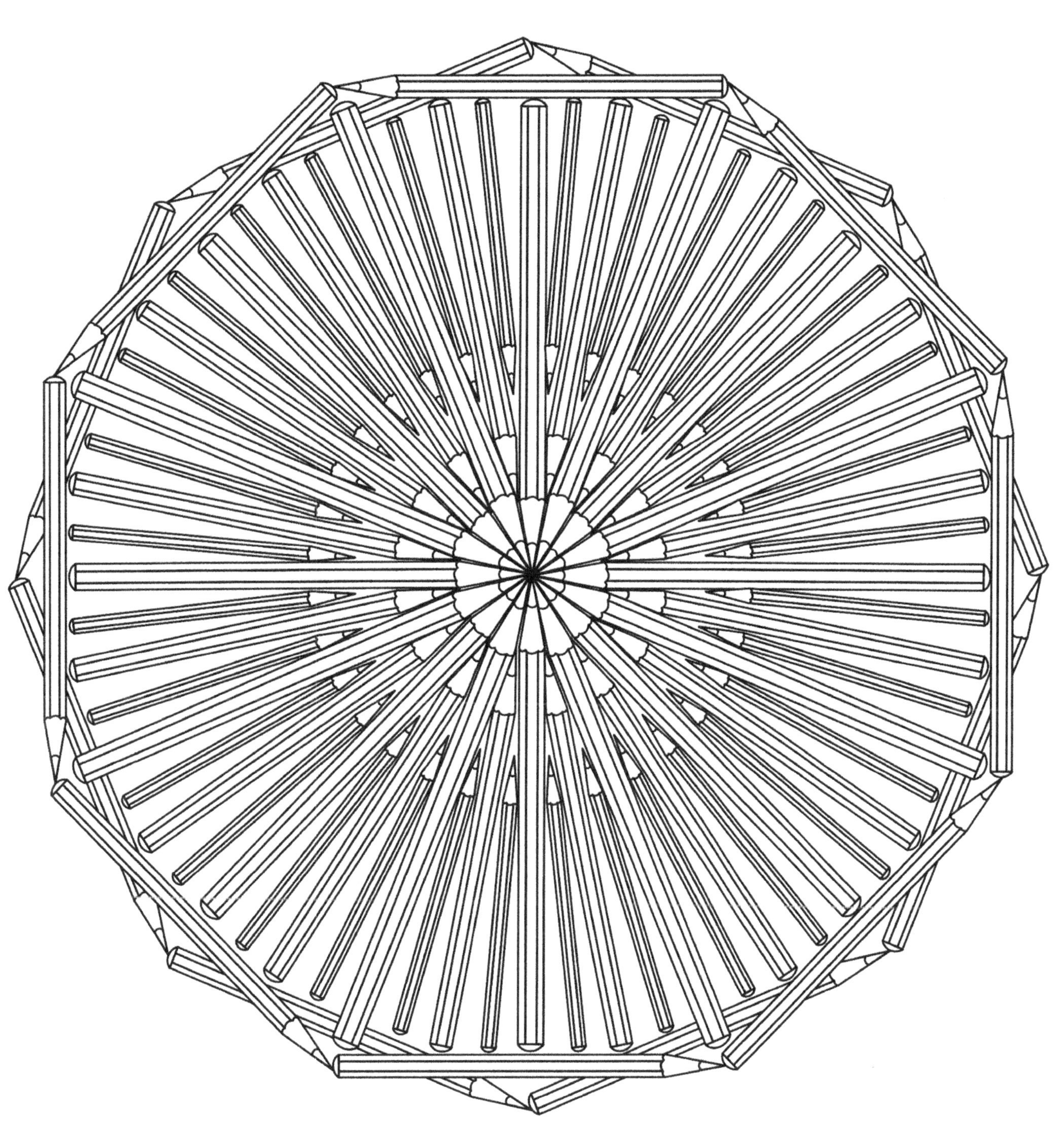

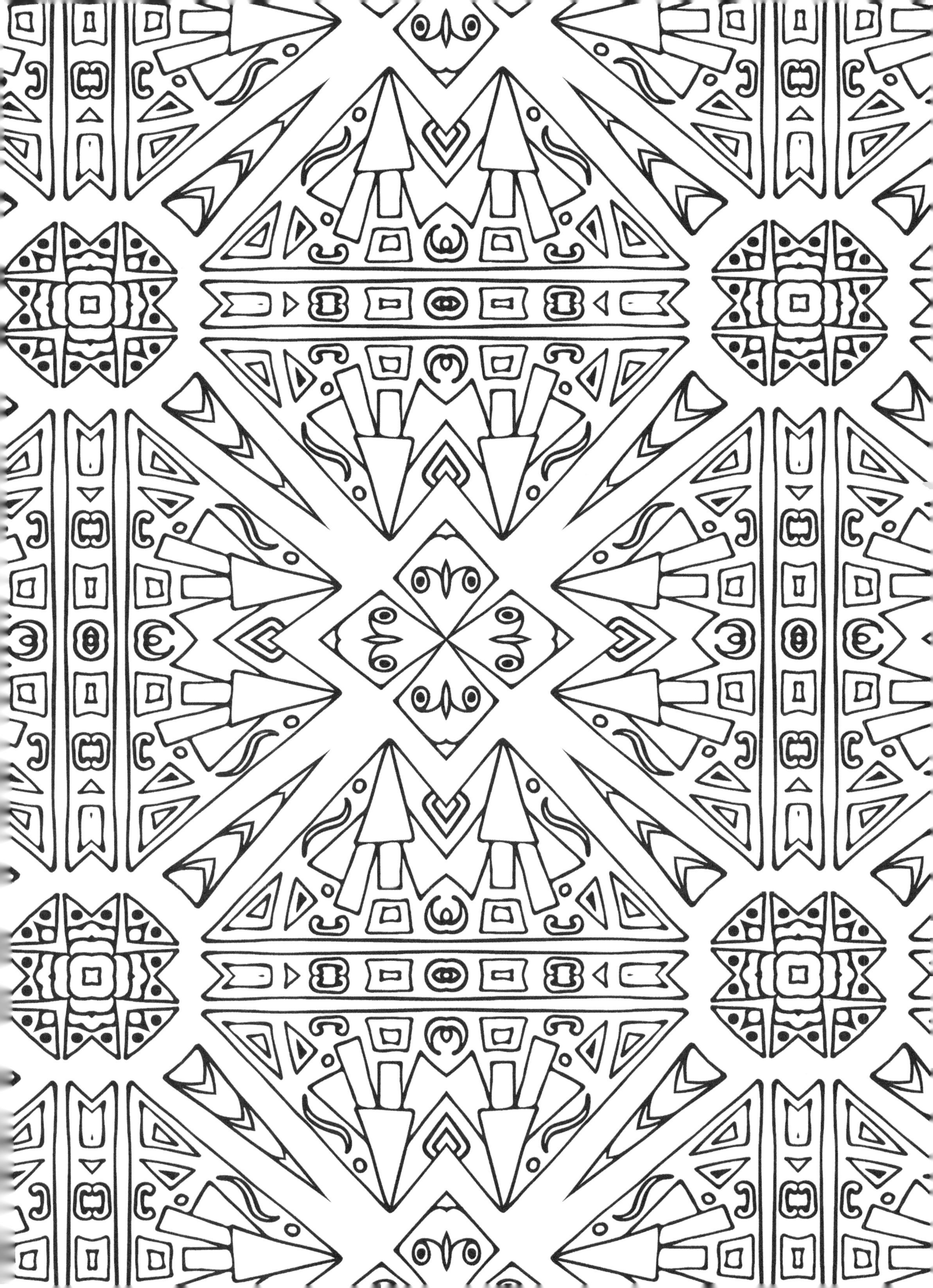

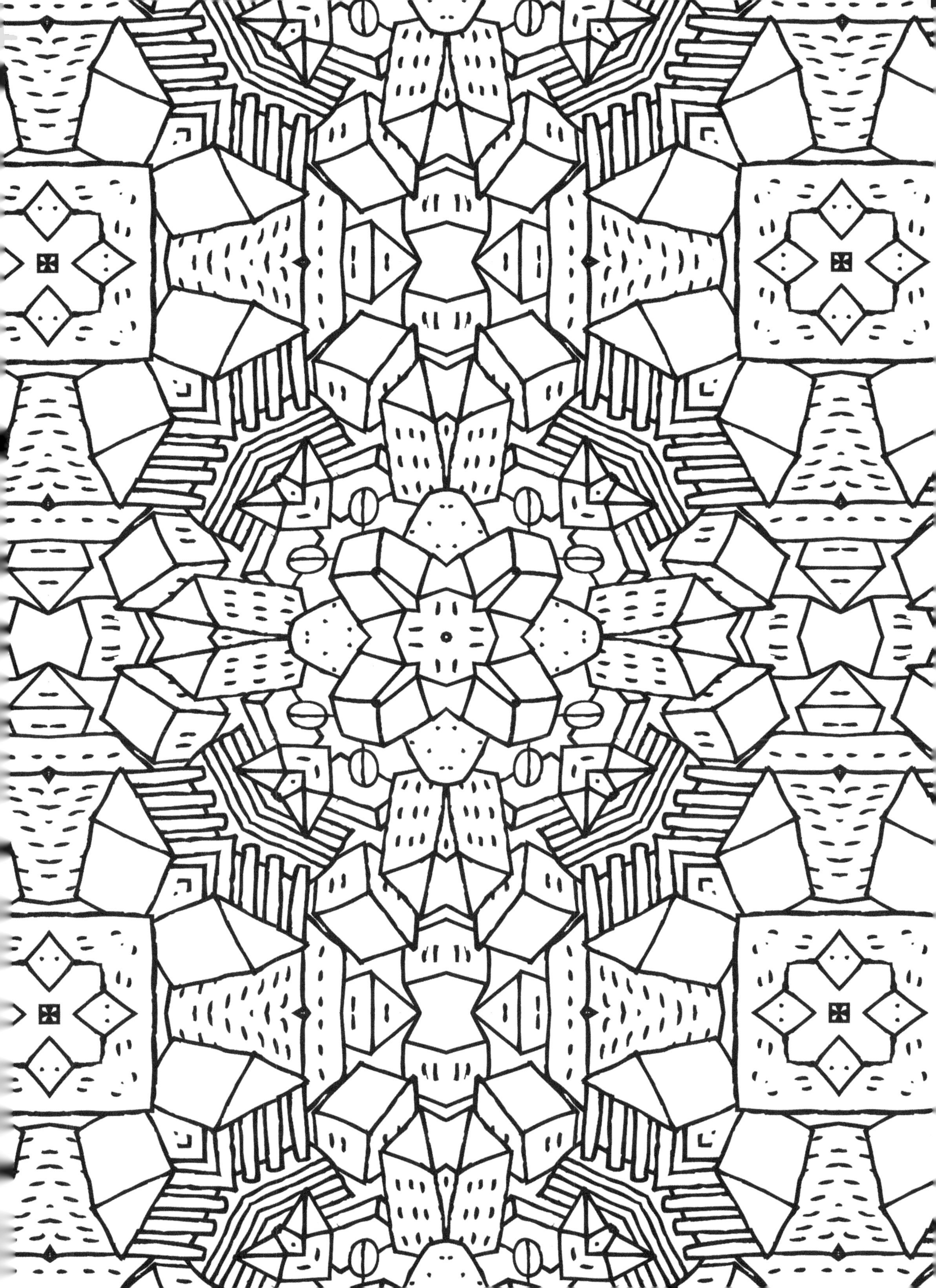

If you enjoyed colouring these designs, then move onto another book in the Progressive Patterns series of Adult Colouring Books.

We are sure you will love them!

We are amazed by the way that each of our designs looks so different when it has been coloured, so please share. We love to see your finished designs, don't be shy, head over to our Facebook page and show us what you have created.

https://www.facebook.com/progressivepatternsadultcolouringbooks

Look out for our other colouring books created by nikk nakk designs.
- Simple Styles
- Decorative Designs
- Intricate Inspirations
- Progressive Patterns Volume 1
- Progressive Patterns - A Man's World
- Progressive Patterns for Lefties
- Fairies and Flowers

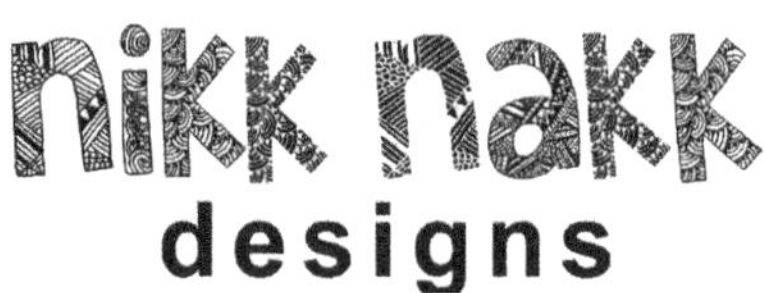

Made in the USA
Monee, IL
07 July 2026